Business Competitive Advantage:
A Handbook for Small Business Owners,
Entrepreneurs and Consultants

Heidi Thorne

First Edition, 2012
Second Edition, 2013 (Updated November 2014, January 2016)

Thorne Communications LLC, USA
www.HeidiThorne.com

Business Competitive Advantage:

A Handbook for Small Business Owners,
Entrepreneurs and Consultants

Heidi Thorne

TABLE OF CONTENTS

Welcome to the New Competitive Marketplace vii

Your Competition 1

CHAPTER 1: Why You Have No Competition 3

CHAPTER 2: Why Everything (and Nothing) is Your
Competition 6

CHAPTER 3: The Monopoly Myth 9

CHAPTER 4: Why You Need Competitors 12

CHAPTER 5: How Your Customers Peg Your Place in
the Marketplace 14

CHAPTER 6: Take the "Competitor Challenge" 16

CHAPTER 7: Why It's Good to Be Near Competitors
....24

CHAPTER 8: "Location, Location, Location" 26

CHAPTER 9: Competitors as Partners? Yes, But... ...30

CHAPTER 10: Mudslinging and Other Competitive
Sports 32

CHAPTER 11: Invisible Competitors 34

Your Customers 37

CHAPTER 12: Customer Matchmaking 39

CHAPTER 13: But Do They Care? 44

CHAPTER 14: Why Surveys Lie 47

CHAPTER 15: Selling a $75,000 Bra? 50

CHAPTER 16: The Follow-Up Fallacy 52

CHAPTER 17: The Customer Switcheroo 54

CHAPTER 18: Situational or Systemic?......................60

CHAPTER 19: Incumbent Power...............................62

Your Pricing and Profits.....................................65

CHAPTER 20: Profits First and Last 67

CHAPTER 21: Pricing Strategies in Marketing..........74

CHAPTER 22: Methods of Sales Forecasting 84

CHAPTER 23: How to Plan for Sales Slumps............90

CHAPTER 24: What is Your Market Share?..............99

Your Customer Service 105

CHAPTER 25: Why "Quality" and "Service" are Not
Competitive Advantages.....................................107

CHAPTER 26: Good Customer Service or Servitude?
....111

CHAPTER 27: 3 Fs to Becoming a Stronger
Competitor...115

Going Forward...117

About Heidi Thorne..118

Welcome to the New Competitive Marketplace

Does it seem like you have a lot more competitors for your small business than you used to? Seems that way for me. Larger companies are expanding their product and service offerings to recoup some of the revenues they've lost due to the economic downturn. Pressing needs of all sorts seem to get those dollars that normally would have gone to you. Unfortunately, as small business owners, if we can't find a way to compete, we will find ourselves out of business.

So we've got to get smarter about our competition and ourselves.

I've been in business for myself for many years selling advertising and marketing products and services. Bigger and more unusual competitors seem to be grabbing bigger slices of my industry's pie, leaving me to wonder who and what was I actually competing against, as well as wonder if I could even compete and continue to build a small business.

So as I re-evaluated how to market a company, I learned a lot about evaluating who my competition really is. I'd like to share some of those insights with you in this discussion on small business competition.

Unlike other business books on the subject which feature the often irrelevant competitive strategies of mega corporations, this book contains real world, practical tips and advice for small business owners, entrepreneurs and consultants. Through discussions and exercises designed to make you think, you'll gain a new perspective on the players, forces, and your place in your marketplace.

What we will not discuss is how to evaluate the size or potential viability of your particular market. That is usually done in a complete business strategy consultation which includes such activities as a SWOT (Strengths, Weaknesses, Opportunities & Threats) Analysis and market research. I recommend that you hire a business strategy consultant to guide you through the process. Having an outside-looking-in perspective is invaluable. (It was for me!)

As the economy continues to present challenges to companies of all sizes, and more companies expand into your market arena, you can't afford to not have a better understanding of yourself and those forces that compete for your customer's dollar.

In this updated edition of *Business Competitive Advantage*, I've added a boatload of resources on handling the sales process including forecasting, calculating and evaluating margins, market share, pricing strategies and dealing with downturns in sales. As with the rest of the book, these segments are written for the real world of small business owners. I think you'll find yourself referring to this handbook often.

So let's not waste another minute and let's get working on your business competitive advantage!

Heidi Thorne

Your Competition

CHAPTER 1:
Why You Have No Competition

When I tell people that I feel I have no direct competitors, they look at me a little bit strangely. But let me tell a couple of stories to illustrate.

Don't Sell So Close to Me

There was a company in our area that was very, very worried about another moving into their territory, one they perceived as a near competitor. Both companies sold the exact same product, identical to the core. However, they really weren't direct competitors, and I'll tell you why.

The concerned company served smaller, onesie-twosie type customers, and the encroaching company served bigger customers, those that would be buying by the pallet or truckload. So, while both companies sold the exact same product, they didn't sell to the exact same customers. So, in that sense, they really were not direct competitors.

Let's take another example. Gas stations sell gallons of milk. Large grocery stores sell gallons of milk. They also both sell gallons of milk for customers' convenience. Gas stations sell it so that they can capture sales from the folks who might otherwise have to stop at a large grocery store for it. Large grocery stores sell it since people are buying food anyway, making it easy to add to their carts. Yet it is unlikely that gas stations will be grabbing any significant "grocery store" market share. And people are unlikely to buy all of their groceries at the gas station quick mart. Again, same product, no direct competition.

Just because you sell the same product in the same geography doesn't mean you're competitors. You directly compete with those who serve an identical customer base and provide a comparable buying experience to yours in addition to those similar or even identical products and services.

Are You a Widget Seller?

In business school, all example companies seemed to sell widgets. Sure, professors use the term "widgets" to generically refer to the products of the company being discussed. But what if you really do sell nameless, generic or commodity widgets?

As you may have noted from my bio, I'm in the promotional product marketing business. Yes, that's imprinted pens, T-shirts, bags, etc. I am in one of the most widget-y businesses out there. A promotional pen from Bic®, is a promotional pen from Bic®. In my chamber of commerce alone, there are at least four or more promotional product vendors. And on the Internet there are thousands of promotional product widget sellers. We all sell the exact same widgets. And I don't feel I compete with any of them.

Really? Really, I don't. Why? I realize that my bundle of products, personnel, processes, promotion and personality make me a totally unique offering. After going through the discussion and exercises in this book, my hope is that you'll realize that you truly don't have any (or many) direct competitors either and understand the unique niche you occupy in your market space.

CHAPTER 2:
Why Everything (and Nothing) is Your Competition

The title of this chapter may sound a little contradictory to the previous discussion we had about having no competition. But really everything can be your competition. Here's how...

I serve a lot of customers that are related to the construction and building maintenance arena, and one of my clients said that they could no longer do business with me. Of course, I never want to hear that, and of course I always want to know why. Basically, the reason that they discontinued doing business with me was because they were given a corporate order from on high that said they either had to cut their advertising (which was what I was selling) or they had to cut a staff member.

How does one sell against that?

It's such an emotionally charged issue. Should I tell them that they would be better off in the long run by buying the advertising than maintaining a staff worker? Truly, and not just for my own personal gain, they would be because it would help them create revenues to retain more workers. But yet, the emotional issue that management had to deal with certainly was difficult, and so I can't even sell against that. Who is my competition here? The staffing and labor relations.

Sometimes you may be selling against a lot of different things. It could be anything. Luckily, in this scenario, the client told me what the situation was. A lot of times they won't even tell you, because either they're embarrassed, or they may not even really understand their needs at that time.

Selling Against Nothing

Here's another scenario that I've run into. In the construction arena, when economic times go bad, it gets really bad for them. So when I was selling advertising in recessionary times, I would be selling against nothing. What do I mean by "nothing?" Doing nothing.

These folks' buying decisions were not between competitors. They didn't have advertising provider A and advertising provider B. They had advertising as one choice and doing nothing in order to save money as the alternative. When the budgets got tight, the advertising went out the window first.

Another competitor related to doing nothing is apathy. Apathetic buyers often do have the need and the funding. They just don't have a reason or interest in buying. It is impossible to sell to an apathetic buyer.

But you may be asking, *"Can't you create demand?"* Honestly, no. Until THEY have a reason to buy from you, they won't. The good news is that apathetic buyers are probably not buying from anyone else either. So you're not out of the running. You're just out of their mind.

So, yes, everything AND nothing can be your competition!

CHAPTER 3:
The Monopoly Myth

A lot of people think, *"Wow, if I was the only provider of the product or service I offer, I'd have customers beating a path to my door."* I'll tell you that's not the case. And I can tell you that from personal experience.

I sold advertising for a publication that truly was the only one of its kind in a marketplace. It was very difficult to sell because I was competing against everything else that they could spend their money on. (Remember our discussion on why everything is your competition?) They would be spending money on expenses such as customer or dealer incentive trips, promotional merchandise, office remodeling, printing and, and... I was being categorized against who knows what. That's a big problem with this scenario.

Sometimes when you're the only and very, very unique provider of what you offer, they don't really know where you fit in their budgeting landscape. I think this is especially the case for selling consulting and other services. There is no such thing as a generic business strategy consultant, pet trainer, lawyer or astrologer. The particular consultant's brand of service and personality truly puts him or her in a monopoly position. While some consulting roles are easier for customers to categorize (such as CPAs) for budgeting purposes, others such as business coaches, might be more tricky. Should that be considered a marketing expense or training costs?

But that's not all. A monopolistic market position does not guarantee sales because of:

- ***Selling Against Nothing.*** As previously discussed, customers are ingenious creatures. Can't get what they need or want due to limited supply or high expense from a monopoly provider? They'll choose something else... or even nothing else.

- ***Desire for Choice.*** Even if a business is masterful at getting customers to buy, customers (and people in general) like to feel like they have a choice, no matter how limited or illusory that choice is.

- ***The Mall.*** The popularity of shopping malls has waxed and waned over the past decades. But the concept is still alive and well. Customers want to feel they have options. If they don't like an option from one competitor, they'll move to the next. And the closer those next competitors are, the more likely that a purchase will be made from one of them. And today we have the ultimate mall: The Internet.

What Should You Do If You Are a Monopoly Provider?

If you are in the situation of being a monopoly provider of the product or service offered, here's the question you need to answer:

*What role or budget category do I want
to fill for my customers?*

Knowing that will help you focus your presentations so your customers can categorize you properly within their budget framework.

Here's an example. When I was selling trade newspaper advertising for a monopoly provider, I would position myself into a marketing consultant role. Since I was presenting myself as a marketing resource, a lot of advertisers would ask me questions about other advertising and marketing investments they were considering. Knowing their bigger picture also helped me in presenting my advertising opportunity to meet their larger objectives. Without taking this approach, I would have easily been lumped with other overhead budget categories such as telephone (for Yellow Pages advertising) or printing.

CHAPTER 4:
Why You Need Competitors

Hearing that you need competitors might sound disturbing to some of you, but let's say this situation happens.

A customer or prospect comes to you requesting a proposal and it's a job that you either can't do, don't want to do, or maybe it's a customer you don't want to serve. You want to be able to refer that person to someone who can do a great job for them. By doing so, you'll be seen as a valuable resource and as someone who is very knowledgeable about your industry and the marketplace as well. Who knows? That customer or prospect might be coming to you for other more suitable projects down the road.

In a later chapter, we'll talk about evaluating the strengths of your competitors. When you encounter unsuitable inquiries or proposal requests, this analysis will come in handy. You might want to even keep a directory of potential competitors for easy reference in these situations.

As we discussed earlier, you don't want to be the monopoly provider of anything. So you need competitors to help take some of the pressure off of you to service unsuitable prospects and projects.

Get a very clear picture about what you provide and what your competitors provide so that you can provide better customer service to your customers.

CHAPTER 5:
How Your Customers Peg Your Place in the Marketplace

Those of you that have followed me for any length of time know that I am a big fan of a certain famous coffee house and, in our area, we have about a half a dozen of those stores. Yes, they all serve the same type of coffee, tea, or other drink product, but they are not the same.

My favorite store has super staff members on board. They take care of you, they're friendly, they get your order done quickly. There's another store in the area that I use just for a quick run to get a drink. They're fast, they're efficient and friendly for the very short period of time that I'm there. Another one is comfortable and close to me. And then there's one that I avoid completely because their staff is not friendly, they're slow on service. But in all cases, the product is exactly the same.

This proves another issue related to competition. Your customers, just like me with all these coffee houses, have pegged you in a certain competitive place in your marketplace... regardless of what you or your competitors believe about market positioning.

Are You Fuzzy?

Because I'm an active networker and offer my expertise on a number of marketing topics to local networking events and groups, my position in the competitive marketplace gets fuzzy.

Evidence? Sometimes when I attend a networking event, I go through my 60-second elevator speech about promotional products and I get an *"I didn't realize you did that! I thought you just did social media."* response from someone I've known for years. Rats!

Before I get too down on myself, I quickly remember that I do address multiple markets and profit centers. So some of this reaction will be inevitable.

If you are in a similar situation, as long as your core market for the particular product in question knows what you do and provide, don't worry about other prospects or markets finding your competitive position fuzzy. You're not talking to them anyway.

Just make sure that all communications with your hottest and most relevant prospects clearly define what you bring to that competitive table.

CHAPTER 6:
Take the "Competitor Challenge"

Old enough to remember the original Pepsi® Challenge? For those of you youngsters who don't, way back around the early 80s, soft drink giant Pepsi would set up blind taste tests around the country to see if people preferred Pepsi to Coca-Cola. Not unsurprisingly, people preferred Pepsi.

Similarly, earlier in the 60s and 70s, one of the most popular ways to demonstrate your product's superiority was through side-by-side comparisons between your product and the "Leading Brand" or "Bargain Brand." (I always wondered where I could purchase Leading Brand and Bargain Brand. *snickers*)

As the years rolled on, and possibly emboldened by Pepsi's audacity, advertisers started naming brands in their comparison advertising. Like the Pepsi Challenge, these marketing efforts set out to "prove" superiority or suitability of one product or service over another.

Tests like these assume there is an absolutely objective and quantifiable way to compare the offering of one competitor over another, as well as to determine which competitor customers will not only prefer, but patronize. Fact is there really isn't.

However, what you can do is a "Competitor Challenge" where you can compare your strengths against those of your nearest competitors. In some cases it might be a Pepsi taste versus Coca-Cola taste comparison. In others, you may be showing how your strength trumps a dissimilar strength of your competitor.

To start thinking of yourself as a unique product within your marketplace, list three existing competing companies that sell the same (or nearly the same) products or services that you do. Include their location and/or website; you want REAL companies, not the fictitious widget sellers from ECON 101 class.

If you're in a new business or thinking about starting a business, this may take some guesswork on your part. But if you've been in business a while, you have some knowledge of what your customers are buying and what vendors they are buying from. Use these real competitors, not who you think they are or should be.

Being able to clearly identify some real potential competitors will help you evaluate where you stand. Suggest reading through the entire exercise and the real-life example that follows before you get started. You'll get a much better idea of what you actually need to do.

For yourself and each competitor, list three strengths each possesses. Notice how I asked you to identify your competitors' strengths as opposed to their weaknesses (so tempting to do, right?). This can be an advantage for you.

Then, for each competitor, I want you to discuss what makes your strengths unique and/or superior to those of your competitors. Are you cheaper or faster? More organized? Have special abilities they don't?

Real Life Example

Here's my example so you can get an idea of how it's done.

I sell promotional products such as bags, pens, T-shirts, etc. imprinted with your logo. Technically, I have LOTS of competitors. While I can't mention specific folks in this book, I can tell you how I evaluated their strengths and those of companies like them.

My Big 3 are:

1. *Large Internet-based retailers of promotional products.*
2. *Printers.*
3. *Sign companies.*

Other than Competitor #1, the online mega retailers, are you surprised that I don't list any immediate promotional product distributors like myself as my competitors? Some of this can be attributed to the fact that for many promotional distributors, including me, these products are one profit center for the business, not the sole revenue generator. Fact is, I run into only a few promo-only direct competitors, primarily at promo conventions.

Your business may be in a similar position. List the most prominent real competitors for your business, the ones that your customers are actually buying from, whether or not they are considered "direct" competitors.

My Strengths

1. *Extensive online shop sites featuring specialty niche products such as domestically sourced.*

2. *Customer education program which includes blog, books, e-newsletter, speaking, etc.*
3. *Vendor knowledge and knowledge of specialty printing processes.*

Competitor #1 (Internet promotional product retailers)
1. *BIG selection on BIG website.*
2. *Speed.*
3. *Large customer service staff.*

My strength in competing against their strength is: *Specialty product shop sites.*

My shop sites, featuring specially sourced product categories that few competitors in my industry touch, are a huge advantage over this competitor who does not delve into these sourcing details in their online catalogs. Customers buying on purpose—i.e. with domestic sourcing issues at the forefront—usually are less sensitive to the customer service niceties and broad selection than other buyers who are simply buying for branding. By narrowing my selection, I helped create and strengthen my market position.

Competitor #2 (Printers)
1. *Can provide direct mailing services.*
2. *Can provide print services such as brochures.*
3. *Long standing reputation in community as "marketing consultants."*

My strengths in competing against their strengths are:

1) Vendor knowledge and knowledge of specialty printing processes; 2) Specialty product shop sites; and, 3) Customer education program.

Except as it relates to a specific promotional product, I don't do print! Every time I've tried to bridge that gap from promotional product seller to provider of print materials such as brochures and business cards, I've gotten burned. I have some, but not expert, knowledge of print. On the flip side, I know printers who venture into promotional products and then get really, really frustrated. It's way more than just hopping onto a database and picking a product from the list. You need to know the vendors and their capabilities. Some of my printer friends have gotten burned with these sales. As well, printing on a promotional product is NOT the same as printing on paper. A whole different animal! So my vendor and specialty printing and product knowledge give me an edge… and a referral partnering opportunity with printers.

Printers are often afforded "marketing consultant" status because they are the first (maybe only) marketing-related vendor that new businesses encounter. So these newbie businesses look to them for purchasing anything related to marketing and/or printing, sometimes for years into the future. There are some printers I know who truly and effectively fill this consulting role. Others not so much. That's where my customer education program can give me either equal footing or even a competitive advantage against some print companies. And, again, referral partnering opportunities are possible.

Competitor #3 (Sign companies)

1. *Quick turn on sign and tradeshow display products.*
2. *Locally produced sign and display products shorten delivery time.*
3. *Customers are already thinking about tradeshows when they contact the company. So offering promotional items at the peak of their tradeshow buying cycle can help get add-on sales of imprinted pens, bags, etc.*

My strengths in competing against their strengths are: *1) Vendor knowledge; and, 2) Specialty product shop sites.*

Very similar to Competitor #2, sign companies are great at making signs. Compared to on-paper printers, though, a sign company's understanding of printing on a variety of surfaces is superior, making them even stronger competitors.

Increasing their market position is the fact that customers are usually connecting with sign companies as they are preparing for events and tradeshows. So the timing issue gives them the competitive upper hand.

Fortunately for me, like printers, sign companies' time to develop promotional product vendor knowledge and relationships is limited. So customers concerned with sourcing issues will likely need to look for companies like mine that focus on that buying aspect. As with printers, this affords a referral partnering opportunity.

Now it's your turn.

My key competitors are:
1.
2.
3.

My Strengths
1.
2.
3.

Competitor #1 (Name)
1.
2.
3.

My strength(s) in competing against their strength(s) is/are:

Competitor #2 (Name)
1.
2.
3.

My strength(s) in competing against their strength(s) is/are:

Competitor #3 (Name)
1.
2.
3.

My strength(s) in competing against their strength(s) is/are:

When you're done with that exercise, put it away and then finish reading the book. When you look at it again after you complete this book, maybe you'll want to add or change a couple of competitors or strengths on your lists. But once you have these things really, really set, you'll want to integrate these strengths into your marketing campaigns and sales efforts to really show how you are different than everyone else who sells the same product or service that you do.

CHAPTER 7:
Why It's Good to Be Near Competitors

Was Target crazy? Walmart had already established a store in a town near my home. But then Target builds a location across the street from Walmart, literally just hundreds of feet away. Why would they do that? Wouldn't the close proximity ignite a head-to-head battle for competitive advantage? Possibly. However, it's more likely that Target understands that being near competitors can bring its own advantages to a business.

How is that possible?

As discussed in the previous chapter, customers like to feel that they have choice, regardless of whether they really do or not. Also, customers want those choices as close together as possible. So Target was providing the community with more choice. If customers have to go trouncing around from town to town (or from website to website) looking for what they want, they may buy what's available. Or, as also noted earlier, they may choose not to buy at all.

Even small businesses can follow Target's lead and position themselves as a contender in the marketplace by using these strategies:

- *Advertising.* Advertising near competitors in print, broadcast and on the Internet, positions a business as an option for customers to consider. (Notice how many different auto manufacturers advertise during one hour of television!) As well, advertising can make even small businesses seem larger than they are and as a viable choice. Nowhere is this more relevant than with Internet advertising.

- *Networking*. Having representation at relevant networking events positions a company as a potential vendor for customers. It also affords an opportunity to make friendly relationships with competitors for either partnering or referrals should the need arise.

- *Strategic Locations.* Most franchises will not locate another franchisee within very close proximity of another for good reason... they're too identical. However, most businesses that are not from the same company do have differentiating aspects that could make closer locations a reasonable choice. However, this should be done strategically and carefully. Hiring a marketing research consultant or business strategy adviser is highly recommended to assist in the process. **Example:** Auto dealers of differing manufacturers often locate near each other—creating a mall of sorts for cars—since they know that customers shop around when purchasing a vehicle.

CHAPTER 8:
"Location, Location, Location"

What does the phrase "Location, location, location" mean? In the real estate business it usually is the response to the question "What are the three most important factors in selling real estate?" No amount of property features such as building, grounds, decorating or price can overcome the negative impact of a poor location which can have a major impact on a business' competitive position. What's interesting is that location issues are of prime importance in other aspects of business including marketing, advertising, sales, management and human resources.

Location Factors in Marketing

Marketing involves bringing products and services to the marketplace to meet a business' revenue objectives. It includes advertising, public relations, sales, packaging, retail placement and promotions. (Advertising and sales will be discussed separately below.)

Where a product or service should be marketed is one of the most important questions that marketing managers must answer.

A marketing issue related to real estate is the location of stores and offices. If in-person customers cannot find the brick-and-mortar location of a business easily, it will less likely to survive, regardless of how appealing the environment, product or pricing are. Location analyses of retail sites are invaluable in finding suitable properties to house a business.

On a smaller stage, place a product in a store location that doesn't attract an audience with the right marketing demographics and it is sure to fail. Even placement within the store itself can make or break a product. **Example:** If a canned product cannot be positioned on an easily visible shelf location, it has a lower chance of being selected by consumers. Thus, marketing managers may offer promotions to retailers to achieve better placement or provide special displays (such as temporary end cap promotional racks) to attract attention.

Getting press releases and articles placed on broadcast media, publications or websites that reach a target audience demographic is the goal of the public relations function. Press located in media that doesn't reach an intended target is akin to purchasing the best property in the worst location. It's still nice, but it won't accomplish anything.

Location Factors in Advertising

Similarly, advertisements placed in the wrong places, too few places or too many places will not be effective.

This analysis begins with the question, *Where are your customers when they are in the market for what you sell?* Home? Car? Work? Vacation? The dentist? The location where people are likely to be making decisions about purchasing will suggest advertising opportunities.

Example: Say the service promoted is teeth whitening. Where would people be when they are thinking about this? First, they might be searching online, making Internet advertising, such as PPC (Pay Per Click), a possibility. Second, they may be in the dentist's office making printed brochures located in the waiting room another viable choice.

For more reading on location factors and the concept of *"where"* in advertising, read *Choosing a Method of Advertisement for a Business* at http://hub.me/aeVC6

Location Factors in Sales

All marketing and advertising is in support of the sales function of a business. Sales efforts add even more location factors.

For online businesses, the "Buy Now" buttons and functions should be logically located on the page to direct website shoppers through the buying process. Some organizations use heat map analysis to determine optimal placement for buttons, advertisements and links on their sites.

For offline sales teams, also referred to as outside sales, analyzing location factors can help sales managers assign geographic territories for maximum return. **Example:** If a large metropolitan region takes three hours to travel from one end to the other to meet with customers, it might be wise to split the region into two parts so that sales reps spend less time in the car and more time in front of customers. As discussed under marketing, location of brick-and-mortar stores and offices can have an impact on sales results.

Similarly, location of a trade show booth at an expo can affect traffic to the booth and the number of sales leads received. Ironically, right by the entrance may not be the ideal location.

CHAPTER 9:
Competitors as Partners? Yes, But...

As a promotional products distributor, I have access to thousands of suppliers for every imaginable item. However, one category of product is still a multi-step, multi-vendor process to complete: T shirts and other promotional clothing. It requires an order from a warehouse, which goes to a contract decorator, and finally gets shipped to the customer.

Some distributors own their own printing and embroidery equipment and do the decorating in house... and have the staff to do it. But that's a huge investment. Since this is a very small portion of my business, I outsource.

Hooked up with a friendly competitor who did a lot of this type of work and did a great job. For years, they handled my orders until they relocated out of the area. When that happened, they also hooked me up with a contract decorating friend of theirs who has done some wonderful work for me.

This is a prime example of how developing friendly partnership relationships with competitors can work, offering opportunities for everyone. But there are some cautions:

- ***Do a Thorough Competitive Analysis.*** Understand what each party is bringing to the marketplace and to the table before even considering partnering.
- ***Only Work with Trusted Colleagues.*** If there is not a relationship of friendship and trust, don't partner!
- ***Create an Agreement.*** Seek legal counsel on creating competitor partnering agreements to cover items such as non-disclosure and confidentiality, rights and responsibilities.

CHAPTER 10:
Mudslinging and Other Competitive Sports

Business owners sometimes fret about competitors making negative statements about them in the marketplace. Yes, your competitors could and might resort to mudslinging.

Now if those negative statements are libelous or slanderous, that's another story. But usually trash talking by competitors centers around how your product, service or whatever is not as good as theirs. Don't get all flustered about it. Those are just their biased opinions. And if the only way they can promote themselves is by tearing down a competitor, they have lost their ability to promote themselves on their merits. Sad.

It's really easy to get bent out of shape emotionally if you hear that one of your competitors is talking negatively about you or your company. It's even easy to slip into defensive mode when you encounter competitors at a networking function and they're telling everyone how great they are compared to their competitors.

Also, if a competitor is "comparing" their offerings to yours, that is not negative. That is merely showing how various competitive options stack up. Example: If a Car

A offers X number of miles per gallon more compared to Car B, that's comparison. However, if Car A's salesperson says Car B "sucks," that's just mudslinging.

Business is a competitive sport. The winnings go to those who are strong contenders and don't engage in unsportsmanlike conduct. You bring a unique package of products, personnel and personality to the marketplace. So you're not really competing one-to-one with any trash talking competitor anyway. Don't succumb to returning fire by spreading negative comments about your competitors.

Remember, also, that it's your customers who are really making the comparisons, not you or your competitors.

CHAPTER 11:
Invisible Competitors

In the chapter on *Why Everything (and Nothing) is Your Competition* we talked about invisible competitors such as a recession, apathy, and labor costs that are taking the dollars that a customer could spend with you. You might want to reread that chapter before doing the following exercise.

For the following exercise, think about three invisible and indirect competitive threats—such as budget items, attitudes or situations—that could be competing for the dollars that your customers could be spending with you. Then decide how you would sell against that or if it's even possible.

Example #1 (major budget item of incentives): I sell trade advertising to wholesalers who offer incentive trips and gifts to their dealers, often with the effect of trade advertising dollars being cut to pay for those incentives. How I can approach the advertiser is by showing how making advertising a part of their incentive budget can help increase awareness of their incentive and help recruit new dealers.

Example #2 (situation of recession, attitude of fear): During the recession, many of my customers became fearful about buying any advertising or promotional products from me. Many just discontinued buying everything. That's a bad strategic move for them that could make it harder for them to recover in the marketplace when the economy improves.

In selling against fear, I can present my products and services as ways to prepare for a successful post-recession period. I could also sell them on less expensive, but still effective, options that help keep their name in front of customers and maintain their marketing momentum.

Example #3 (attitude of apathy): Doesn't matter what the economy is doing, an apathetic buyer is my worst customer prospect. They just don't see any need for my advertising and marketing products and services. Heck, they've *"been in business a long time and never needed to market."* That's not really true, of course. But I realize it's all about perceived need. Also, many of these are DIY (Do It Yourself) marketers. My way to sell to them is not to sell to them. I might keep them on an email or mailing list so they know I'm still around. But other than that, it's "Next!"

Now let's take at a look at your invisible competitors. 3 major budget expenditures, attitudes, or situations you may, unknowingly, be competing with are:

1.

2.

3.

The ways you will present your product or service against each of these invisible competitors are:

1.

2.

3.

Your Customers

CHAPTER 12:
Customer Matchmaking

Looking for a perfect customer match? Like the online dating services, you'll need to create a profile of all the qualities you're looking for in a customer.

What you're looking for is a demographic and behavioral profile of your ideal customers. Sure, lots of people can buy from you, but not all of them are a good fit for you. Ideal customers are the ones that are the easiest and most profitable for you to serve.

Here are some factors that determine your ideal customer profile:

- *Income/revenue level*
- *Geographic location (by country, region, state or ZIP code)*
- *Type of organization or individual (i.e. schools, young families, seniors, associations, industry)*
- *Organization size (i.e. small business, multinational corporation, single-person households)*
- *Ability and/or willingness to buy*
- *Purpose for buying this product or service*
- *Previous use or purchase of the type of product or service you sell*

- *Age of population or business*
- *Annual income or revenues*
- *Personality (i.e. no nonsense, creative, adventurous)*
- *Hobbies, sports or leisure activities*
- *Educational level*
- *Membership in various associations*
- *Attendance at relevant trade shows, conferences and events*
- *Subscriptions to magazines of topics related to your industry*

This list is not exhaustive. Try to think of all the ways your ideal customers are unique from other buyers. Bottom line is, don't just consider the classic income and geographic demographics or, for B2B markets, business size, location and classification.

Interestingly, even your customer base can be a competitive factor! Think of those companies that claim they are such-and-such supplier to the stars. By doing so, they're usually saying that they serve the elite Hollywood set, a definite differentiator. Or think of the ads that claim their products are preferred by busy moms. They're not trying to appeal to extreme sports athletes. Your appeal to particular markets, particularly specialty niches, can give you a competitive edge.

Additionally, what populations may be viable prospects today, may be totally irrelevant next year. Monitoring shifts in demographic profiles is a key marketing function.

For a more in-depth analysis of your customers and what, when, how, where and why they buy, check out my other book, *SWAG: How to Choose and Use Promotional Products for Marketing Your Business*. In it I thoroughly discuss my Promo With Purpose concept which helps you analyze your customer's buying scenario.

Business Customer Profiling

Businesses are also often grouped by their Standard Industrial Classification (SIC) or North American Industry Classification System (NAICS) codes. SIC codes were developed by the Occupational Safety & Health Administration (OSHA) of the United States Department of Labor. NAICS codes are those used by the U.S Census Bureau. These codes are assigned to businesses by the various government agencies, not by the businesses themselves.

The list of characteristics that combine to create an ideal business customer profile can be many! Though there are many qualities that could define any business no matter the size, targeting a group of customers by one quality only can waste marketing dollars, time and effort.

For example, businesses that could be classified under SIC Code 2052 Cookies and Crackers could be a massive packaged cookie manufacturer OR a small business that makes custom cookies for serving at weddings and events. Sure, both businesses use ingredients such as flour, eggs, and sugar to bake cookies. But they would differ dramatically in areas such as these:

- *Scale.* One may use truckloads of flour, the other may purchase bag by bag for custom orders. A manufacturer may need multiple shifts of workers, whereas the small business may be just one person.

- ***Marketing.*** A packaged goods manufacturer may market and advertise locally or even nationally and have wide distribution to the consumer markets. The custom cookie maker is more likely to be local and market to either event planners or end users.
- ***Location.*** A manufacturing operation for commercial cookie baking could be a massive factory. In the custom market, the "factory" could be a small business owner, home oven or rented out kitchen facilities.

Savvy marketers look well beyond the industry code when establishing their ideal customer targets, even though they may start with the all encompassing industrial classification. When purchasing mailing and sales lead lists, or when doing their own research, marketers can choose several of the business demographics characteristics to filter it to just those who are most likely to become buyers.

Using the cookie makers example, a supplier of bulk baking ingredients for large scale manufacturing could filter their marketing targets based on these factors:

- SIC Code 2052 Cookies and Crackers
- Commercial factory locations of a certain square footage
- Revenues that would be typical of the size of factory targeted
- Geographical locations to which ingredients could be cost-effectively shipped

That's only four major filters. There could be several other factors unique to the supplier's offerings on which the list could be further filtered to get to a group of prospects that are a good customer match.

CHAPTER 13:
But Do They Care?

Remember when everyone was trying to "go green?" I do. And since that whole going green thing aligns with many of my personal values, I became an expert of sorts on eco friendly promotions. Offering green products seemed to align so well with the zeitgeist, and almost none of my direct or near competitors were even focusing on green. I thought this would give me a clear competitive edge.

Ramped up a blog on eco friendly promotions. Focused my main shop site on green products. Talked with customers and networking connections about it. And then, drum roll please… nothing.

I got a few customers who wanted to show their greenness with reusable bags or recycled pens. But the results were dismal at best.

Then a different kind of "green" issue reared its ugly head: recession. I had one client bluntly tell me that if there was a five or ten cent difference between a standard product and an eco friendly version, she would go with the standard product every time. Love good honest feedback.

As you evaluate your strengths and those of your competitors, ask yourself if your customers and prospects really care about this unique strength of yours. If they don't, it's not truly a competitive advantage. In this case you're faced with three choices:

1. *Find a strength within your company that they do care about.*
2. *Find a customer base that does care.*
3. *Reframe your product or service offering.*

With my green issue, I could have chosen to pursue an environmentally concerned customer base such as conservation groups and companies working on sustainability initiatives. But that wasn't really panning out well either. Many of those groups were shunning promotional products altogether in order to go greener.

So now what? Had to take a hard look at what was actually selling and why.

One of the other groupings of items I had included in my product lineup was items manufactured in the United States. Domestic sourcing can be a green aspect since it eliminates overseas shipping which can be environmentally costly. I had also included them because I do a lot of work with markets, such as unions and the trades, which are sensitive to American made issues.

What I found as I looked at my Google analytics was that people were finding my shop sites through organic search because of these American made items, to the tune of 20 percent of my shop site traffic at times. Hmm...

Today, a large chunk of my business is focused on U.S. made products. Do I still include green options? You bet I do. But I include American-made recycled, reusable and biodegradable products within and alongside my normal U.S. made offerings. Essentially, I have reframed them as domestically sourced.

Look carefully at what your analytics, financial data and customer feedback are telling you because they can be indicators of a hidden competitive strength you have.

CHAPTER 14:
Why Surveys Lie

Ask your customers why they buy from you and you may get one of the following: 1) Answers that are so odd you question whether you really know these people; 2) Some amazing and maybe surprising feedback; or, 3) Shrug of the shoulders.

Sometimes customers don't consciously know or remember why they buy anything from anyone. They've done it for so many years they've forgotten. Or buying was dictated by someone else so they're just following orders. Or you're a friend of theirs. Give them a "rate this item on a scale of 1 to 5" survey and they'll often just fill in or click any answer that fits with their mood for the day or so they can finish and get a discount coupon code for participating. Or they'll just blurt out some generic answer such as "good service."

Personally, I like the surveys that ask if the participant buys a certain product or service from a list of potential vendors, as well as ask them if they have purchased in a certain timeframe such as three or six months. While participants can lie like they do on most surveys, these types of questions cause them to think a little harder about their answers. These questions also help you steer the participant into providing the competitive information you are seeking.

An Easy Survey to Discover Your Competition

Create a two-question survey for your customers and prospects that will help you obtain information about who your competitors really are. You can offer some sort of reward or discount for completing. But if you tell people in advance that it is a two-question survey that will take them less than one minute to complete, they may be more willing to participate, regardless of reward.

You can do these in person, as paper surveys or use one of the easy online survey tools.

Example Questions

1. Have you purchased [*fill in your company's product or service*] within the past [*fill in desired timeframe such as 3 months, 6 months, 12 months—whatever is appropriate for your product or customer buying cycle*]?

   ___ Yes

   ___ No

If the buyer answers no to the first question, the survey is done. You want information from people who have actually purchased a product or service similar to yours. Create a thank you screen that explains that the survey is seeking information from people who have recently purchased and encourage them to participate in future surveys. If they end the survey, give them the discount code or some other reward that is different from those who complete the entire survey.

2. Who did you buy [*fill in your company's product or service*] from? Check all that apply.
    ___ Competitor #1 Name
    ___ Competitor #2 Name
    ___ Competitor #3 Name
    ___ Other _____

Create a check-off list of as many potential competitors as you can. Do NOT put them in alphabetical order. Showing a random order list can encourage participants to read each entry more carefully. Allowing "check all that apply" and write-in "Other" answers will also help you identify more potential competitors.

That's it. What will you gain from this survey? First, you'll know if your target market is actually buying. Second, you'll know who they are buying from. Sure, you could ask them why they bought such-and-such from various competitors. But you'll usually just stress out your participants and won't get valid feedback. Just knowing who really is in your market space is a huge piece of competitive intelligence.

What if you get lots of "no" answers to the very first question? That still is valuable. What this could signal is that your target or current market is not as viable as you had hoped. If you are asking them about purchases of a brand new product or service, this could also signal that you have a lot more missionary sales work to do. Carefully evaluate whether you have the resources to do that. But again, that is important competitive intelligence for you.

CHAPTER 15:
Selling a $75,000 Bra?

Around the holidays, a lot of you may get that lingerie catalogue that features a bra encrusted with diamonds and semi-precious stones that has an astronomical price tag of maybe $50,000 or $75,000. Now the market for that bra is extremely limited. I'm sure that the markets for your products and services are not that narrowly focused, but serving a limited market is very challenging.

For example, I've served a market where the core group of buyers or potential buyers had access to co-op marketing funding. I was selling advertising which could be paid for with those co-op funds. As I veered farther and farther away from that group, a group who did not have that co-op funding, it became very, very difficult to sell to them. I had to do more promotion, had to do more sales calls. So it really became less and less profitable the farther away I got from that core limited market.

The other challenge with limited markets is that if that limited market falls apart, your sales and your business could fall apart too. So what you really have to ask yourself is, *"How can I repackage what I sell for a different type of market?"* Doing so will create multiple streams of income and multiple markets, helping you create a sustainable business for the future.

For example, I sell the same product to two dramatically different marketplaces. They have different service levels and delivery requirements. But I'm actually selling the exact same product to both.

CHAPTER 16:
The Follow-Up Fallacy

If you've been in sales for a while, you have heard the advice, *"If you don't follow up, you don't get the business."* In principle, that's true. But as I look over my records, you know what I found? Sales usually don't close for a lot of reasons that have nothing to do with my follow-up, my customer service level, my product, my pricing, my proposal, anything like that.

It's often a million reasons that have everything to do with the customer. They have gone into a completely new direction. They have lost funding. They have decided to back-burner the project. They have decided on a product or service I don't even offer. It's just tons of reasons that have nothing to do with me or my follow-up. Rarely is it a *"We went with Competitor B because they were cheaper."*

While you keep chasing these people down and annoying them, you're saying no to following new leads and inquiries that could close.

It is a real time management tool to decide at what point you are going to let these people loose. Depending on your particular sales cycle, if after the first couple follow-ups they haven't closed on the sale, it might be time to move on or just to keep in touch with them, maybe a couple months from now.

What you have to remember is that YOUR sales deadline, no matter how important it is to your business, is not the customer's deadline. He does not care about your sales goals and quotas. To believe otherwise is also to buy into the notion that you have magical sales and persuasive powers. Once you have made your best effort presentation or offer AND asked for the order (something a lot of people are afraid to do), it is in now in the customer's hands and agenda.

What I hope you'll take away from this discussion is that while you can continue to improve your presentations and offerings, buyers' decisions are not always based on you. So quit beating yourself up and move on. Don't keep chasing business that won't close.

CHAPTER 17:
The Customer Switcheroo

Have you ever been the victim of a customer switcheroo? I have. Here's how the customer switcheroo works. You're doing business with a company and things are rolling along. Then one day you get a phone call or email that says, *"In the future, you will no longer be working with Joe, but you'll be working with Jane."*

Now that could be really good news, especially if your relationship with Joe was sort of so-so. It's a new opportunity for you to build a stronger relationship with Jane and with the company.

But if you've spent years developing a good working relationship with Joe, you might see the return on your sales investment and future revenue opportunities disappearing almost instantly. I've had this happen a number of times with various clients. You then have to start the building process all over again. Ugh!

Not only is it crushing to your sales success, it can open up a whole new set of competitors that you previously did not encounter. Why? Your new contact may already have a posse of preferred vendors that they will usually turn to instead of you. Double ugh!

The Dreaded Information Gatherer

Worse yet, what often happens in a customer switcheroo is that they pass off the handling of my business to a staffer who has no authority, no decision-making ability, and usually no experience buying what I sell. So my sales efforts become an education process of this new person. Say hello to the dreaded "Information Gatherer."

And gather they do. I had a situation where I was working with one of the company's owners. Then suddenly he asked that I call on his "marketing manager." Come to find out it was the company's receptionist who was given a gentrified title (I don't know many marketing managers who man a switchboard).

This gal had absolutely no clue how to buy promotional goods and services. She would send me photos of items from home that she liked and then wanted me to source them for her. Usually that's not a problem if it's close to an item that we normally carry on our shopping web sites. But after about the sixth totally off-the-menu custom item request, I told her that I would have to begin charging my usual custom sourcing fee per item searched. That was the last I heard from her or the company.

The other way that Information Gatherers can be devastating is that, due to their inexperience in buying what you sell, they turn to a variety of vendors. And these days, that usually means they go hunting on the web. Then they want you to compete with whatever yokels they find in cyberspace. Apples-to-oranges competition, ugh!

Information Gatherer alarms should also start going off when it comes time to sign off on the contract and you get an *"I need to talk to my manager"* or *"They're not ready to buy yet"* (for the umpteenth time).

My favorite story here is the one where I was working with the company's owner who asked that I call on his daughter who was his "marketing manager." (Seeing a pattern here?) I bluntly asked her if she had the authority to go ahead with purchases. She answered yes. Then, miraculously, in the exact same sales call, I asked if she could make a decision on a particular purchase because we were running short on time. Answer? *"I need to discuss this with my dad."*

What to Do with the Switcheroo

While this situation may be temporary, it could be permanent. But you may not know right away. What should you do?

Initially act on the assumption that your new contact does and will have the authority to do business with you. You will exhibit confidence in this person which can help the newcomer feel more comfortable working with you. But do take some time to explain how you have worked with your old contact and the company in the past so that the new contact is not put off by your particular brand and level of service. Then observe the new contact's behavior over the next weeks and months and adjust your selling to meet the client's changing needs and priorities (especially if you realize you've been dumped on an Information Gatherer).

If it is abundantly clear that you and your business have been demoted to being handled by an Information Gatherer, explain to the new person how you have worked with the company's previous contact and assure her that you are available to assist with their purchases. But be very clear about buying procedures. If necessary and you have the resources and systems to do so, you might want to downgrade the account to one that can be handled on a "retail" level (such as through an online shop site, counter sales, packaged consulting services, etc.). Adopt a passive keeping in touch strategy (e-newsletter, mailers, an occasional phone call) to monitor the situation.

For example, I have several higher maintenance "consulting" level accounts that have cell phone and in-person access to me and I have one-to-one contact with the company's top management or advisors. If at some point they turn me over to administrative personnel that have no authority or buying expertise, I will then steer these new contacts to my shop sites where they can merrily search for promotions on THEIR time and THEIR dime, not mine. As well, I have a blog, book and e-newsletter which can help educate them if needed.

Death by M&A

Mergers and acquisitions. While they can salvage or strengthen either or both parties in the deal, something always dies in the process. When the economy tanked, I saw a lot of my sales relationships get killed off in these company ownership changes.

Usually, the stronger of the two companies determines the vendor relationships for going forward. Here's a scenario that I had.

I had been selling promotional products to a division of a larger company for a number of years. In addition, I offered them a lot of marketing tips and ideas. We had a great consulting relationship.

Then they merged with another company. The first year or so after the merger, things ran pretty much as usual except that we had to keep changing logos and such over time. But then the inevitable customer contact switcheroo occurred.

My new contact bluntly told me that, *"Corporate buys all that stuff from XYZ Big Box Internet retailer."* I can't even compete with XYZ, nor do I want to. At least I have to thank them for telling me who my new competition was. But this account's history with me is history.

What should you do if you find yourself selling in a merger or acquisition situation?

I've noticed that during the transition phase, purchasing comes to a halt until the dust settles. So adopt a keeping in touch strategy with remaining or new contacts because the newly formed entity may become disenchanted with current vendors during the turbulent merger and acquisition phase. They also may have some changes in personnel as the merger goes forward which could present some opportunities for you.

Often, though, it's a slow-go and is not going to produce anything in the near term. Again, it could be a starting from scratch selling situation. Adopt a more passive keep in touch strategy to monitor until new policies, procedures and personnel are more established.

Really, the only strategy that you have for dealing with all of these switcheroo scenarios is to keep filling your sales pipeline with new leads and inquiries so that you're not dependent on these pieces of business that have reached their end.

CHAPTER 18:
Situational or Systemic?

Another area you need to think about is the customer and their current business situation. You have to decide whether the reason they are not buying from you is situational, such as what I had with the downturn in the economy for the construction arena, or if it is systemic.

If it's situational, you know that is a temporary scenario. That could change down the road. With them you want to use a keeping in touch type strategy, maybe connecting every three to six months or annually (depending on your typical sales cycle), just to see if their situation has changed.

But if it's systemic, they might buy from you once, but they're not loyal clients. Or they absolutely will not buy from you. They will buy anything else but what you provide. When and if they do buy, they just are doing it because either they're forced to, or maybe one of their competitors is doing the same thing, or maybe they landed some unexpected cash and don't want to lose it to additional taxes. But they don't really believe in the products and services that you are offering.

Again, even for systemic non-buyers, I'd suggest an annual update, just to see if there's been any change. A lot of times a systemic non-buying status might be dependent on who's in that decision making position. I've had the situation happen where I've had a really great client contact for years. Then that person moves on to a new job, either with the same company or outside the company, and the successor just doesn't believe in what I'm offering or doesn't believe in me, or both. But then the next successor is just the opposite. Luckily, after serving the same marketplace for well over a decade, I was able to watch the process and get a better understanding of what was happening.

Another systemic problem is obsolescence. Your product or service may not be advanced enough for certain markets. That's just a natural sales life cycle. Realize where your offerings are still viable and hone in on those markets. On the opposite side of the desk, your customers may be in an industry that is on the wane, and they know it. So they might be winding down operations and have limited buying ability. Unless you're a turnaround expert, it's unlikely they'll be customers of the future.

Assuming your product or service is typically a good fit for this customer, and their non-buying behavior can be attributed to a current situation they find themselves in, keep them in your possibility pool. If they're not buying because it's not a good fit for you or the customer now or in the future, it's time to move on.

CHAPTER 19:
Incumbent Power

In elections, the incumbent elected official usually has the advantage because of "the devil you know syndrome" where people would rather vote for someone where they know what to expect than an unknown entity.

We have the same situation with vendors for your clients. They would rather deal with a vendor that they've done business with for quite a while because they know what to expect. It's really difficult to get into those types of clients where they've been doing business with a particular vendor for a long time.

Here's another incumbent situation which is virtually impossible. It's where a family member or a good friend is the vendor for a product or service that you sell. For example, I have a client that buys advertising from me. I noticed he uses promotional products at shows. So I approached him about it and he said, *"Well, it would be nice to do business with you, but my sister is in the business."* So unless his sister leaves the business or they have a family falling out, chances of me getting in there to sell promotional products are not high.

What you want to do in those situations is adopt a keep in touch, keep it friendly strategy with them. Keep them on an email list. If you see them at events, say hello. The objective is to keep your name in front of them for when the buying time or situation might be right.

One day you might realize that you've become an incumbent vendor for your clients. Nice! Then customer service issues become uppermost. Plus, these clients are often more receptive to new ideas that you present because you're part of their team. Your current customer base can be a goldmine of sales potential. Incumbent clients are powerful, too!

Your Pricing and Profits

CHAPTER 20:
Profits First and Last

Profit margins that are needed for a business to survive (or thrive!) are primary metrics that both business owners and sales personnel must know. Profits must be the first consideration, even though it's the last number on one of a company's primary financial documents: The profit and loss statement. (That's why it's also called the *"bottom line."*)

There are a number of methods of calculating profit margin. Each method provides a different metric that helps businesses make better decisions. These calculations all begin with the profit and loss statement.

What is a Profit and Loss Statement?

A profit and loss statement (often referred to as a *P&L* statement) is a report of a business' operating gross income, cost of goods sold and overhead expenses... in that order.

- ***Gross Income.*** Gross income is all the money that a company receives from sales or other income from the operation of the business. Miscellaneous income such as interest on bank accounts is typically not included in this figure since it is not a product of the business' operations.

- **Cost of Goods Sold.** Also known as *COGS,* these are all the costs that are incurred to produce the products and services of the business. Materials needed to make a product would be an example.

- **Overhead Expenses.** Unlike COGS, overhead expenses are all the costs that are incurred to run the business. These are not directly attributable to production of products or services. Items would include utilities, payroll, telephones, etc. Some of these costs are fixed and others are variable. **Important:** In reporting, note if the total overhead expenses are BEFORE or AFTER taxes. In other words, do they exclude (before tax) or include (after tax) taxes? Both before and after tax metrics should be monitored since taxes can be a huge annual cost that must be considered. Consult an accounting professional to determine an estimated tax rate based on current and applicable tax laws.

Using these three numbers, the profit margins for the business can be calculated.

Calculating Gross Profit

Gross profit, whether in dollars or percentage, is the amount of profit before overhead expenses are deducted. Calculating gross profit margin is done using the following formula:

Gross Income - Cost of Goods Sold = Gross Profit

The result is the gross profit in dollars. This is an important metric, but for sales forecasting, COGS and gross profit in percentages are more useful:

Cost of Goods Sold ÷ Gross Income = Cost of Goods Sold Percentage

Gross Profit ÷ Gross Income = Gross Profit Margin Percentage

Unfortunately, many business owners and salespeople only look at gross profit when making decisions. What's most important is net profit.

What is Net Profit Margin?
   Net profit is the amount of money left over after COGS and overhead expenses are deducted from the gross income. The formula for net profit in dollars is:

Gross Income - Cost of Goods Sold - Overhead Expenses* = Net Profit

Then to figure the net profit margin as a percentage, one formula is:

Net Profit ÷ Gross Income = Net Profit Margin %

For sales planning, overhead expenses are usually also expressed as a percentage, calculated as follows:
Overhead Expenses* ÷ Gross Income = Overhead %*

Two easier net profit margin percentage formulas for sales and planning use, that come up with the same answer are:

100% - COGS % - Overhead %* = Net Profit Margin %

OR

Gross Profit Margin % - Overhead %* = Net Profit Margin %

This makes is easier to calculate when preparing quotes or evaluating performance. See discussion and examples later on in this article.

* As discussed earlier, whether this amount is before or after taxes should be noted. Having both figures on hand is useful.

Putting It All Together

Now that the necessary numbers have been calculated for profit margin assessment, how are they used for sales forecasting and planning?

In general, COGS expenses vary with the level of sales. Conversely, overhead expenses are often incurred regardless of the level of sales. So every sale must contribute to funding overhead. This is frequently overlooked by many in sales, causing them to quote and discount inappropriately.

Some examples will help illustrate. We'll be using the second net profit margin formula for sales use noted above which is:

Gross Profit Margin % - Overhead Expense % = Net Profit Margin %

Example 1:
- Gross Profit Margin = 60%
- Overhead Expense Percentage = 30%

Plugging this into the formula, the result would be:

- *60% - 30% = 30% Net <u>PROFIT</u>*

A result like this would indicate an operation or sale that makes a profit.

Example 2:
- *Gross Profit Margin = 30%*
- *Overhead Expense Percentage = 60%*

Plugging this into the formula, the result would be:

- *30% - 60% = (30%) Net <u>LOSS</u>*

This business or sale is losing $0.30 on every dollar it makes and will likely go out of business if it cannot either or both: 1) Boost gross profit margin; or, 2) Reduce overhead expenses.

Winning Sales and Losing Business

As is obvious from the preceding examples, it is possible to be making sales, but losing business. Therefore, sharing profitability needs and targets with all sales personnel and relevant staff is essential.

Some businesses are afraid to share their overhead percentages with staff members and sales teams. Yet, by not doing so, they are encouraging their teams to make day-to-day decisions that could cripple the business. As well, sharing an overall overhead percentage is unlikely to divulge any confidential financial information.

In businesses where sales quotes and estimates are the norm, setting both gross and net profit margins for sales personnel to meet on every sale is critical.

Avoid Robbing Peter to Pay Paul

Merely looking at the net profit margin in dollars for the entire business can hide the fact that losses from some profit centers or sales are being absorbed by others, in essence creating a *"robbing Peter to pay Paul"* scenario. Should the profitable center of the business be discontinued, the business could sustain heavy losses or even go out of business.

If all sales, regardless of source, are being lumped into one big total, this lopsided scenario is much more likely. Prior to being able to accurately forecast sales, a business needs to segment and track the income from each of its profit centers. If this has not been done in the past, it can be quite a project to sift through historical sales receipts and determine sales for each center, although the exercise can be very enlightening and helpful.

Similarly, COGS for each profit center needs to be evaluated since lower costs for some products may be hiding very high costs for others.

What is needed to avoid this situation is a separate P&L statement or report showing the net profit margin for each profit center.

What Do *"In the Red"* and *"In the Black"* Mean?

In many accounting programs, a net loss on a P&L statement is shown in red ink to call attention to it. Thus, when a business is *"in the red,"* it means it's sustaining losses.

If a business is experiencing profits, a net profit is shown in black ink on the P&L statement. So a business that is *"in the black"* is doing good... maybe. As noted in the segment *"Avoid Robbing Peter to Pay Paul,"* even a net profit can hide losses within the business.

Trivia Fun Fact: The Friday after Thanksgiving in the United States is frequently referred to as *"Black Friday"* because that is when many retail businesses go from being *"in the red"* to *"in the black."*

CHAPTER 21:
Pricing Strategies in Marketing

Next to forecasting sales, setting pricing strategies in marketing a product or service is one of the toughest jobs facing small business owners and sales and marketing managers. Actually, pricing and forecasting are related efforts that need to be coordinated to help preserve and build profit margins.

Following are some of the most common pricing strategies.

Competitive Pricing Models

Matching what competitors are offering as prices is a strategy often pursued by larger organizations who can absorb some losses from offering less than profitable pricing, usually to gain higher market share. Products and services offered at these rock bottom prices are referred to as loss leaders. This strategy banks on the hope that customers will make additional purchases at retail or above OR make aftermarket purchases in the future. **Example:** Ink jet printers are offered at super low prices so that the manufacturer can make money on the printing cartridges in the future.

Businesses who use competitive pricing strategies may start out using MSRP (discussed below). But then they carefully watch what their nearest competitors are offering for the identical (or very similar) offerings, adjusting pricing to either match or come close to that of others. If the business is a large enough retailer (such as Walmart or Target), continuous pricing adjustments of this type require significant technology and administrative investments which are usually out of the range of small businesses.

While it is important for businesses of all sizes and types to have knowledge of prices in their marketplace, competitive pricing can be one of the most financially dangerous pricing models. Totally basing prices on competitors can kill a business' profits even to the point of going out of business. So this strategy is usually pursued by large companies that have a large array of products and services to offer which can offset losses from discounting or price matching.

MSRP Pricing Strategies

Businesses who purchase goods or services for resale may choose to use the manufacturer's suggested retail pricing (MSRP) as their pricing structure. This makes it easy for the business to set prices, but evaluating whether the price meets the business' profit goals is a bit more difficult.

These businesses are usually given a discount off the MSRP as a wholesale price. The difference between the MSRP and the wholesale price is the gross profit margin.

Overhead and a desired profit margin need to be deducted from the gross, as noted in the following example.

Example: A company receives a 40 percent discount off of MSRP to purchase goods from a manufacturer for resale. Therefore, 40 percent is the gross profit margin. The company has an overhead rate of 25 percent and desires to retain at least a 10 percent profit margin after costs. Working the numbers...

40% gross profit margin - 25% overhead - 10% minimum desired net profit margin = 5% net profit margin

So in this example, the company could discount the MSRP by 5 percent and still retain their minimum desired net profit. Alternatively, they could choose to stick with the MSRP as the price and boost their total net profit margin to 15 percent.

But say that the MSRP is 30 percent. Here's how it changes the scenario:

30% gross profit margin - 25% overhead - 10% minimum desired net profit margin = - 5% net profit margin

In this situation, the company is losing 5 percent on every sale. Solutions they can pursue include: 1) Reduce the desired net profit margin that they want to 5 percent; 2) Increase the price they charge customers by 5 percent; 3) Reduce overhead; or, 4) A combination of all three strategies.

The first option reduces the net profit the company earns. The second option preserves the net profit margin but may receive some market resistance if customers are used to paying a lower price for the product. The third option requires a critical review of expenses to identify possible cuts. However, if the cuts reduce the level of customer service, it could have an effect on sales. And while doing a combination of reducing expectations, increasing prices and reducing overhead may be beneficial, it may be difficult to figure which of the strategies is actually helping to preserve profits.

Markup Pricing and Cost Based Strategies

Developing prices based on cost is a little tricky to understand at first, but it is truly just a process of plugging in the numbers. Cost based pricing, also known as markup pricing, is usually done for products, but can be used for services in combination with other pricing models.

What causes confusion for most people is the fact that markup is NOT the same thing as gross profit. For example, to achieve a 50 percent gross profit margin, the markup is 100 percent. Markup is the amount that is ADDED to the net cost to create a retail price.

Desired gross profit margin needs to be determined BEFORE determining a markup. Critical to finding a profitable retail price is determining an adequate gross profit margin. This is a combination of overhead costs plus a desired net profit margin. Remember gross profit margin is the amount of revenue left over after net cost of goods sold (COGS) is paid.

So a starting point for determining a gross profit margin would be finding the desired gross profit margin:

Overhead Percentage + Desired Net Profit Margin Percentage = Desired Gross Profit Margin Percentage

To figure a retail price that achieves the desired gross profit margin, this formula is used:

Formula #1: *Net Cost of Goods Sold / (1 - Desired Gross Profit Margin) = Retail Price*

While this formula works every time, it is unlikely to be one that can be easily used by sales and service staff when preparing quotes. Usually, the markup percentage (or multiplier) is given to them. The basic formula for arriving at a markup rate is:

Formula #2: *Gross Profit Margin Percentage / (100% - Gross Profit Margin Percentage) = Markup Percentage*

So to arrive at a retail price, the long formula is:

Formula #3: *Net Cost of Goods Sold + (Net Cost of Goods Sold X Markup Percentage) = Retail Price*

Applying a little algebra to the equation, another way to solve for retail price is:

Formula #4: *Net Cost of Goods Sold X (1 + Markup Percentage) = Retail Price*

In the equation, the term (*1 + Markup Percentage*) provides an easy multiplier that staff can use to quickly calculate a retail price from net cost.

Formula #5: *1 + Markup Percentage = Multiplier*

The multiplier can also be expressed as a percentage. For example, a markup percentage of 25 percent would create a multiplier of 1.25 which is the same as 125 percent.

Example: A company has a 25 percent overhead rate and wants a 15 percent net profit margin. The net cost of an item that they resell is $6.00. Determine the retail price and what multiplier they would give to their sales team.

25% + 15% = 40% Desired Gross Profit Margin

Formula #1: *$6.00 / (1 - 0.40) = $10.00 Retail Price*

Using a markup pricing model, the retail price would be calculated as follows:

Formula #2: *40% / (100% - 40%) = 0.40 / (1.00 - 0.40) = 0.6667 OR 66.67% Markup Percentage*

Formula #5: *1 + 0.6667 = 1.6667 Multiplier OR 166.67%*
Plugging in the multiplier…

Formula #4: *$6.00 X 1.6667 = $10.0002 Rounded to $10.00 Retail Price*

As shown above, both formulas result in the same retail price. The multiplier formula is just easier to use. So to make a 40 percent gross profit margin, this company would have to multiply their net costs of goods sold by 1.6667 or 166.67 percent (a 66.67% markup).

Surprised at how much a product needs to be marked up? In the example, **that's more than 1.5 times the net cost.** This is a concept that most customers and, unfortunately, many small business owners have difficulty grasping. Being in business means more than just paying the net cost for a product.

Is an 80 to 94% Markup Fair?

In an online forum, a participant was upset at what was noted as an *"80 to 94% markup"* on equipment and supplies charged by a construction and maintenance contractor. The participant had found the parts online for a much lower cost. I answered that in business it is often necessary to charge 2 to 3 times the net cost of the item to maintain profitability. The response to my answer was that "excessive markup" could be the reason many small businesses fail. Fair or fail?

First, let's clarify what 80 to 94 percent markup really means. Using the formulas and solving for markup, it would mean that the multiplier would be 180 to 194 percent. Sounds like a lot, eh? Heck, that's almost 2 times the net cost!

But let's look at the most important number: gross profit margin.

Algebraically solving Formula #2 to obtain the gross profit margin, we find that an 80 to 94 percent markup translates into roughly a 44 to 49 gross profit margin. That may even sound like a lot to some until overhead is factored in. In some businesses, overhead can be as high as 25 percent of revenues or more... sometimes way more. This can quickly obliterate any profit margin. And if taxes weren't included in the overhead, bam!, that profit margin can be almost wiped out.

The business in question in the forum was contracting. Contracting can be an overhead cost intensive business due to vehicles, administrative costs, phones, dispatch, insurance (huge bill!), tools... the list goes on and on.

So whether any markup percentage is fair truly depends on the business and the costs to run it.

Value Based Pricing Models

How should prices be set for services, particularly unique services such as custom consulting projects? This is one of the toughest pricing scenarios because it is not usually based on costs, but on the value of knowledge, experience and expertise.

Using competitive pricing can be a slippery slope toward becoming unprofitable in custom service businesses. For example, good writers can be paid very handsomely for their skills. However, low cost content sites online can offer written content for only a few dollars per project. Competent writers who lower their prices to compete with these sites devalue their expertise and quickly become frustrated or financially strapped.

But the question remains as to how to price services based on value. The following are some strategies that consultants and other service providers may use as a starting point for setting service pricing:

- ***Employment Equivalent.*** Some professionals who make the leap from employment to offering their expertise on the open market use their employment salary as a basis for what to charge customers. An annual salary would be divided by an annual number of hours based on standard work week (50 weeks X 40 hours = 2,000 annual hours). This could work if services are sold to clients similar to the previous employer who may wish to outsource various functions. If not similar employment history is available, looking at industry reports for salaries in similar professions can also provide a baseline hourly rate. The caution is that it may not properly cover the expenses of offering these services as a business. So a thorough evaluation of expenses needs to be done prior to setting an hourly consulting rate.

- ***Need.*** How much is needed to maintain the business and the lifestyle of the owners? Some consultants figure what they'll need to survive both professionally and personally, set that as a goal and then set hourly rates to help meet those goals. A realistic forecast of the number of jobs that can be sold is critical to setting a rate that meets all needs.

- ***Custom Project Quoting.*** Many service and consultant business projects are custom quotes since each project is unique. A custom quote could be a combination of MSRP, markup and value based pricing.

Justifying what may seem as higher prices for services requires that the business build a reputation and brand name that builds brand loyalty and trust.

Are You Really Selling "Perfume?"

The cost to manufacture perfume can typically be a small fraction of what is charged. So what is a customer actually paying for?

Perfume, though actually a physical good, follows a value based pricing model. The value comes from the design, packaging, advertising and the way customers feel when they wear it. That last factor actually has the biggest value. People want to feel attractive and want to associate with the gorgeous celebrity models or designers pitching the product. Ironically, the higher the price, the more people desire it.

If your product, whether it's a physical item or a service, is one that makes people feel special, look beyond the cost and markup factors when pricing. Are you pricing your "perfume" high enough to make you, your company and your offerings desirable? Something to think about.

CHAPTER 22:
Methods of Sales Forecasting

Ask any sales manager or small business owner about the most difficult duties of their job and you're likely to hear projecting sales and profits. Methods of sales forecasting used can vary depending on the business.

So much depends on being able to accurately project what income will be coming into the business. It can determine if additional staff can be added, if projects can be pursued and, most importantly, if the business can meet its financial obligations to employees, vendors and owners or shareholders.

Sales Forecast versus Sales Goals

Is a sales forecast the same as a sales goal? Not necessarily. A sales forecast is a realistic prediction of what a business can achieve in terms of sales revenues. Sales goals, on the other hand, could be set higher than forecast to motivate sales personnel. However, some businesses do set both the forecast and goals to be the same amount.

Historically Based Sales Forecasting

If a business has been in existence for a number of years, a track record of sales will be available to reference. If no major changes to the market or the business are anticipated, it is relatively easy to predict that sales results will be similar for the coming year. The forecast, then, is simply plugging in the past sales figures as projected revenues for the following year, plus (optimistic forecast) or minus (pessimistic forecast) a small percentage.

Historically based forecasting is often used for businesses with large volumes of transactions, particularly those with smaller per sale dollar amounts. **Examples:** Restaurants, retail.

Forecasting Contract Business

Businesses such as consulting, real estate, construction and manufacturing typically sell on contract.

Contracts that are somewhere within the approval process, with revenues projected to be realized in the coming year, are usually included in forecasts. These include:

- *Contracted Sales.* Any customer contracts that have been signed and will be fulfilled in the coming year.
- *Tentative Sales.* Contracts that have been submitted, but not yet signed and accepted by the clients. Typically when a sale is at this stage, it has a greater chance of actually occurring and is usually included in a sales forecast.

However, these contracts may not include all business that's anticipated to be received in the following year. Additional forecasted amounts could be based on historical sales data.

Forecasting Sales in New Businesses, Changing or Unknown Markets

When no track records exist because a company is experiencing dramatic and sudden market changes, entering a new market, or the business itself is new, sales forecasting is much more akin to gambling than science!

In these difficult cases, the following can be used to help build a forecast:

- ***Sales for Similar Operations.*** This can be difficult if not impossible to obtain, especially for independent small businesses, but may be available for businesses such as franchises where franchisors regularly track this data. The sales results for the similar operation can become the initial forecast for the new franchise.
- ***Breakeven Analysis.*** Looking at the projected cost of goods sold (COGS), expenses and investments that a new business or venture will incur can create a breakeven revenue level that needs to be met to keep the doors open. During the first year or years, sometimes achieving breakeven can be quite an accomplishment! This is due to the higher investments in such things as advertising, equipment and personnel needed to get it going. Forecasting sales for breakeven, plus

any additional sales that the business feels it can achieve, might be a place to start.

During the early years of new and changing businesses, adjustments to sales forecasts (upward or downward) may need to be made in response to results throughout the year in addition to annually.

Forecasting Sales Growth

Forecasting sales growth should be based on factors that could legitimately increase sales, not wishes or intuition. These could include:

- *Promotional advertising.*
- *Increased sales staff or activity.*
- *Anticipated changes in the business or marketplace that can positively impact sales.*

For projecting growth due to increased advertising or sales activity, anticipated response and conversion rates can be used. Response and conversion rates from previous efforts can be used to forecast additional sales for new campaigns. If no track record exists, it will be difficult to make this determination. In those cases, industry standard responses can be used. **Example:** Direct mail response has often been noted as having a rule-of-thumb response rate in the range of 1 to 2 percent. Not all of those will ultimately buy, of course. But projecting sales growth of maybe 1 percent for a direct mail campaign might be realistic.

For increased sales efforts, a business can rely on past sales-call-to-sales-closed ratios to determine what would be a realistic forecast. **Example:** If a business knows that for every 10 sales calls it makes, one will lead to an actual closed sale, it can more easily determine what results might be realized from increased sales activity.

The additional number of sales anticipated would then be multiplied by the average sale to determine a realistic forecast for growth.

Forecast versus Actual Sales

Sales forecasts are usually done annually at minimum, being reviewed quarterly, monthly, weekly or even daily depending on the business. In response to changing situations, forecasts may be revised. Though there may be exceptions, for small businesses, usually weekly or monthly reviews are an adequate minimum review interval.

It is unlikely that sales, no matter how carefully forecasted, will exactly match actuals. Any major deviations, whether positive or negative, from the forecast should be investigated for probable causes. What qualifies as a major deviation can vary with the business and industry. For some, even a couple percentage points deviation could be devastating event or a cause for celebration.

Possible causes for deviations from forecast could be any of the following:

- *Overly optimistic or pessimistic forecasting*
- *Tentative or even contracted sales that did not materialize... and why they didn't.*
- *Unexpected events such as weather disasters which can either decrease or improve sales depending on the business (e.g. home improvement stores may experience additional*

sales when storms cause property damage to an area).

- *Unexpected or unusual sales that are not expected to repeat in the future.*
- *Problems with sales or service personnel or systems.*

In addition to reviews of forecast versus actual sales for the current year, actual sales are usually compared with the same periods in the previous year to identify possible trends. This is where noting major deviations is helpful. **Example:** An HVAC business had a July sales figure that was 30 percent ahead of forecast due to an unusually hot and humid summer. If this year's July sales were 30 percent down when compared to those of the previous year, it would not be seen as problematic. It was seen as a result of an unusual weather condition that is not a trend.

Once anomalies are identified, a more realistic and reliable forecast for the following year, based on actuals, can be developed.

CHAPTER 23:
How to Plan for Sales Slumps

Aargh! The sales didn't meet forecast. Now what? Will this trend continue? Or is it just a temporary blip? Discovering the cause of any drop in sales is key to developing strategies for coping with the situation, particularly for small businesses. Read on to learn how to plan for sales slumps by determining the underlying causes.

Seasonal Slumps

Some products and services have a seasonality aspect to them that will naturally create sales peaks and valleys throughout the year. While the lows can be very low (maybe even zero) at times, the peaks make up for it. Examples of businesses that can experience this type of sales cycles include: *swimming pools, Halloween costumes, HVAC services, travel and construction.*

Even though business owners and sales managers are aware of the cycle, it can be very unsettling since overhead expenses keep accruing regardless of sales. The good news is that if peaks and valleys are relatively predictable, sales forecasting is a whole lot easier.

Sales Strategies:

- ***Know the Peaks and Valleys.*** Though this may be difficult for brand new businesses, those that have some sales track record should have a better idea of which months are peaks and which are valleys. Knowing when these might occur can help in planning promotions, staff and facility requirements.

- ***Set Aside Reserve Funding for Downtime.*** Refer to the company's monthly profit and loss statements to determine overhead expenses throughout the year. Plan to place in a reserve savings account an amount equal to or greater than annual total overhead. This helps eliminate stress and can prevent the need to access emergency loans to cover such items as payroll. Even if it's just the small business owner that gets paid as would be the case in many micro businesses, a reserve can keep the business going without dipping into personal funding.

- ***Offer Preseason, Post Season and Off Season Sales Promotions.*** Preseason promotions can help get anticipated peak periods off to a great start. Post season deals can squeeze some last revenues from the market before heading into a slump. Off season deals can help fill in the slump periods though they are unlikely to buoy sales to peak levels.

- ***Offer In Season Promotions with Caution.*** There is no reason to offer promotions and discounts while demand is high. However, some businesses do so to push the sales peak even higher. In season deals should be kept to a minimum.

- ***Use Downtime to Retool.*** Every business, no matter how efficient and effective, needs downtime to recover. This is especially the case in peak-and-valley businesses which can stress out staff, systems and facilities during peak periods. Plan productive activities for downtime such as facility improvement, sales and staff training, software and website updates and other improvement projects.

Long Sales Cycles

Similar to seasonality, sales cycles can also cause sales slumps. This is particularly the case in large, commercial B2B (business to business) businesses and complex sales such as industrial equipment, transportation and long-term consulting projects. Some deals could take years to close if the dollar value is extremely high. **Examples:** jet airliners, commercial real estate, government projects and custom software design.

Since the volume of orders may be small while the dollar values are high, forecasting is usually based on contracts that are existing in-house or tentative. Historical sales levels, along with published industry indicators and reports (such as the McGraw Hill Dodge Reports for the construction industry) can be used to estimate additional sales.

Sales Strategies:

- ***Understand the Sales Cycle.*** Monitoring how long it takes from initial inquiry to actual closed business is an important metric for forecasting slow or long sales cycles.

- ***Set Aside Reserves for Longer Periods.*** Unlike annual seasonal sales slumps, these sales could take years to close. So reserves to cover overhead expenses for multiple years needs to be set aside to avoid the need for debt to keep the business alive. How many years will depend on the specific sales cycle.

- ***Develop a Lower Cost or Alternate Offering.*** To fill in gaps between large projects, some businesses offer second tier or alternate product and service lines. These can be stripped down versions of primary products whose sales could generate larger sales inquiries in the future. Or these could capitalize on company strengths which could migrate well into other offerings. **Example:** Communications systems that can handle security surveillance. With this strategy, carefully evaluate whether the cost to develop an alternate product line will produce enough return and avoid cannibalizing the main line that causes a *"robbing Peter to Pay Paul"* scenario as discussed earlier.

Obsolescence and Technology Trends

A company can manufacture the finest desktop PC computer in the world. But with technology marching to an ever more mobile device beat, the desktop computing market is in decline. This is an example of technological obsolescence which will, inevitably, cause a sales slump.

The technological marketplace is littered with stories of failed companies who pursued *"building a better mousetrap"* in favor of innovating.

Usually companies with *"cash cow"* products (those with high market share, but low future growth) can easily be lulled into thinking the market will remain that way for years. Unfortunately, as technology developments come along faster and faster, it is unwise to not be looking to what's next.

Sales Strategies:

- ***Identify When an Offering will Become a Cash Cow and Seek Greener Pastures.*** Monitoring sales figures over a long period of time will usually show a sales increase as a product gains popularity, stagnation and then decline. Using graphs to track sales over extended periods of time can help easily identify when a profitable product may be heading into decline. Innovation must become a top priority even when sales are at their peak for a profitable product.
- ***Dump the Duds.*** Discounts and promotions on aging product lines can help forestall the inevitable sales slump. Be aware, though, that it is easy to mistake these promotional sales as a sign of renewed interest.

Changes in Customer Attitudes and Preferences

Changes in customer attitudes and preferences can torpedo a company's sales quickly. Examples would include environmental and product safety issues that sway customers to purchase alternatives or eliminate the purchase altogether. **Example:** Plastic baby and water bottles that contained BPA (Bisphenol-A) were left on store shelves when news broke about health concerns related to BPA.

Sales Strategies:

- *Subscribe to Relevant Blogs and News Sources for Your Industry.* These publications, whether in print or online, can be valuable in identifying threats to sales on the horizon. Be prepared to push other product lines or pursue new ones.
- *Watch Consumer Trends.* For general consumer trends, read and subscribe to trend watching sources online.

Economic Downturns

Regardless of how well a business is run or marketed, a poor economy can cause slumps that can close the doors in a hurry. The Great Recession late in the first decade of the 21st century made this a reality that many businesses now need to face.

Sales Strategies:

- *Monitor Economic Trends.* What is ironic is that in the early years of an economic downturn, some businesses will still be doing very well, maybe even excellently. This can trick business owners and sales managers into thinking that economic changes will not affect them.
- *Prepare for an Extended Slump.* As with seasonal or sales cycle slumps, setting aside funds to keep a business going during a downturn

should be done as soon as possible. This will help ensure survival.

- **Limit Promotions.** Also ironically, promotions to help boost sales during recessions and other economic downturns can actually have a negative rebound. Cash strapped customers now become used to receiving a much lower price and/or perks, making raising prices later very difficult.
- **Hold the Line on Profit Margins.** The knee jerk reaction to economic troubles is often to lower prices. Like unwarranted promotions, price reductions can eat into a company's profit margin to the point of being unsustainable.

Population Shifts

Shifts in population—global, national, regional or local—can upend a business literally forever. And it's not just a question of number of people; the demographic mix can also completed change a customer base. **Example:** If a college town has a significant and continued drop in student enrollment, local restaurants could suffer. Conversely, if the college has a huge rise in student population, restaurants could experience increased sales or even growth.

Sales Strategies:

- **Watch Population Trends.** Monitor census data for shifts in the general population makeup and regional trends.
- **Prepare to Divest or Invest in Response.** Certainly adjust sales forecasts in response to changing demographics. But carefully evaluate

the long term effect of the shift on sales. If the market is shrinking, and will continue to do so, changing or eliminating company's offerings that are no longer viable may be the best answer. If the shift is deemed temporary and the market will rebound, or the market is anticipated to grow, then investing in preparation would be appropriate.

Sales Personnel and Service Changes

Changes in systems, facilities, procedures and personnel can cause sales slumps, particularly while changes are being made and new personnel are getting acclimated to their new jobs. This is especially the case when new salespeople come on board. They need to get to know the market and the market needs to get to know them before any significant sales volumes are realized.

Sales Strategies:

- ***Have a Sales Training and Mentoring Program in Place at All Times.*** Some salespeople change jobs quickly to take advantage of greater compensation packages either at other employers or with the same employer. This can leave gaps in sales territory coverage which can be devastating. So having a solid sales training and mentoring program in place can help provide a line of succession should an inevitable opening occur.

- ***Have Realistic Expectations for New Sales Personnel.*** Being the "new guy" is tough! Not only do new personnel have to learn a new job, they need to learn a new culture and market, too. This will certainly have an impact on their performance. Setting achievable goals for the first year can help get launch a satisfying and successful start for all.

- ***Alert Customers of Changes in Personnel, Procedures and Places.*** Put new sales or service people serving customers who have high expectations can be frustrating for both parties. Same for changes in how and where things are done. Posting *"Please Be Patient With Us While We're Improving Our Service to You"* type notices in service areas or on websites can help diffuse some of the frustration for everyone and keep sales from walking out the door.

CHAPTER 24:
What is Your Market Share?

Market share is the amount of revenues that a company generates compared to that of the total revenues for that market. But what makes up a "market?"

A market is the collective of all companies offering the same or similar products and services. It can also be companies serving the same or similar customers. A market area can be further broken down by one or more of the following marketing demographics:

- *Geography*
- *Individual product categories or models sold in the area*
- *Type of region (city, suburban, rural, residential, retail, industrial or commercial)*
- *Type or size of business served*
- *Age (of consumers or businesses)*
- *Gender*
- *Industry*
- *Household dwelling type or size*
- *Or any other demographic that helps to define the subject market*

Calculating Market Share

Market share is calculated by first determining the total revenues for the particular market being studied. Determining this figure can be the most difficult part of the calculation. This figure can be obtained by the following methods:

- *Primary Research.* A company or organization can hire a consultant or research firm to study a market and determine its size and revenues. Consulting firms can also do these studies on their own and sell the research.

- *Industry Associations.* Many industry associations commission studies of this type regularly for their membership. This research may be posted for public use, for members only or it may be available for a fee.

- *Government Studies.* The U.S. Census Bureau, Small Business Administration and other national, regional and local government agencies regularly do research of markets for economic planning and reporting purposes. Many of these studies are available online for free.

Since any of these studies are done annually or less often (some major census studies are only done once a decade!), total market revenues are often a rough estimate. Using the most recent and reliable data available helps improve the accuracy of the estimate.

Once the total market figure is determined, the formula for determining a particular company's market share is simple and straightforward:

Company's Annual Revenues ÷ Market's Total Annual Revenues = Company's Market Share

Why is Market Share Important?

Market share, comparative to the total market, can be a determinant of whether a company is growing, stagnating or losing ground. Though it can be done more frequently, an annual review is usually sufficient for most small to medium sized businesses.

Knowing how competitors rank and how much of the market they control should also be considered to determine how viable it would be to pursue a greater share, as well as what marketing strategies would work best.

- *One or Few Dominant Competitors.* In many markets, there are a few dominant players (sometimes just one!) who command the greatest share of total revenues. In this scenario, smaller businesses are unlikely to have the resources to gain significant ground and may often be unable to compete on pricing. These smaller players would be better advised to pursue a niche marketing strategy to differentiate themselves. **Example:** Discount retailing where mega retailers Walmart, Target and Amazon command large shares of the market.

- *Many Equally Matched Competitors.* When the majority of businesses in a market are equally matched in terms of resources, size, offerings, marketing approach, etc., the market share distribution could be quite evenly distributed as well. Minor changes in market share can be a huge issue and will likely be monitored closely. Because of the similarity among competitors, customers can often quickly and frequently hop from competitor to competitor. Therefore, marketing programs encouraging brand loyalty can be helpful. **Example:** Cellular phone providers which all offer the same phone devices and services.

- *Large Number of Competitors Without Significant Market Share.* In these markets, there may be hundreds or even thousands of micro or small businesses competing. Their offerings may be similar or completely unique. Competitors may not even be monitoring (or caring about) market share. Marketing strategies usually focus on their unique business model, products, personnel or other factors.... and may not even address how they compare to their competition. **Example:** Individual crafters selling online.

Market Share Ranking

One of the other measurements of market share done by researchers or associations are studies ranking various competitors in a particular industry or market. The data can be either collected from public sources or from surveys.

This information helps everyone in the market understand where they rank and what it might take to move up the market share ladder. **Example:** A company who has the third largest market share would know what revenues the number one competitor has, helping them create a sales goal that could help them move closer to the top spot.

This is more than just a egotistical pursuit. Companies who have higher market shares and revenues are much more likely to survive and sustain their participation in the marketplace.

Your Customer Service

CHAPTER 25:
Why "Quality" and "Service" are Not Competitive Advantages

When you ask either business owners or salespeople what separates their companies or product offerings from their competitors, two common responses are "quality" and "service." What are the two most ineffective words you can use in your advertising? You guessed it, "quality" and "service." Why? Because they define everything and nothing at the same time.

Let's look at quality first. In common language use, it typically refers to superior quality. But, technically, quality means a state or condition of something. So when you say you have a quality product or service, what quality are you talking about? Here are some possibilities:

- *Material or assembly that is free of defects*
- *Heavy or light weight, depending on which is preferred*
- *Durability*
- *Correct sizing*

- *Smoothness or roughness, depending on which is preferred*
- *Brightness or lack thereof*
- *Special handling or handmade*
- *And...*

Then let's consider service. What do you mean by that?

- *Delivered fast or within a specified period of time*
- *Inexpensive*
- *Number of staff attending to an order or project*
- *Answering of telephone on first ring*
- *Fully functioning self-service website*
- *Clean restrooms*
- *Convenient parking*
- *Order pick-up at your office*
- *Clean, uniformed staff*
- *And...*

Again, what are we talking about?

A real life example: At our house, we have two vehicles of the same make, purchased from two different dealerships. So when it comes time to bring them in for warranty prescribed maintenance, I bring mine back to the dealer I purchased it from, even though it's about twice as far. Why? Because of the "service."

At my dealership, a friendly uniformed service manager greets you in the service lane, he discusses the maintenance to be done, and directs you to the waiting area where there is quiet, comfortable seating with desks, Internet access, brand name coffee available, and restrooms that I wouldn't mind having in my home. Then, at the time the service manager specified, he comes to the waiting area to discuss what was done and lead you to the checkout.

Contrast this with the other dealership. First, you don't know if you've entered the right door for maintenance services. The parking lot is so small, two cars can barely get through one lane. Noisy, chaotic waiting area with only bar stools to sit on for two hours or more. Then, finally, they call your name so you can escape.

Both dealerships say they have excellent service, yet that "excellent service" is very different in each. The one where I bring my vehicle should probably describe their excellent service in their marketing with something to the effect, *"Relax in our clean, comfortable lounge area while we work on your car. Free Internet, Wi-Fi access, and freshly brewed coffee while you wait. You'll be on your way in 90 minutes or it's on us."* The other dealership, well, they better think about that one.

Asking yourself what you mean by quality and service will help you in presenting that story to your customers in your advertising. For the following exercise, I want you to find five words or phrases that describe your company's "quality." Then do the same for "service." By doing so, you'll have a much clearer way to communicate your competitive advantage.

My company's "quality" can be described as:

1.

2.

3.

4.

5.

My company's "service" can be described as:

1.

2.

3.

4.

5.

CHAPTER 26:
Good Customer Service or Servitude?

Ever heard the Nordstrom tires story? The "legend" says that one day a customer wandered into a Nordstrom store to return a set of snow tires. Even though Nordstrom does not sell tires, they gladly refunded the money. (Google "Nordstrom Tire Story" for more details.) This story has been repeated *ad nauseam* in books and presentations as a role model of customer service.

Certainly, Nordstrom is a retailer that has gained a superstar status for putting customers first. But is this a story that can provide a blueprint of good customer service and brand loyalty programs for others to follow? Probably not. Why?

While this behavior might (emphasis on "might") "wow" any customer who realizes that the company has gone out of their way, it can easily morph from customer service to servitude. Service is providing what it equitably paid for; servitude is being enslaved by customers and their unrealistic demands.

What are customer service traps to avoid?

Dealing with Customer Return Thieves

The Nordstrom tire story can take on a painful twist for businesses who sell on a retail basis. With no quibble, no time limit return policies, some customers have taken this as an open invitation to steal or "borrow" goods from the store. **Example:** A customer will purchase a dress or outfit, wear it to a party or event, and then return it for a full refund.

With the potential for this to happen, why would any business offer overly generous return policies? Because they understand human nature. People who make a purchase and know it has a long or unlimited return possibility, will think that they will return it at some point in the future. Then they go on with their overwhelmed and distracted lives, forget about it and may never return it. That's good news for retailers.

There's no doubt that customer-friendly return policies can help build customer satisfaction and confidence. But these cautions need to be kept in mind:

- *Watch Return Rates.* If return rates become excessive and erode profit margins significantly, changes in policies should be considered.
- *Ask for Return Feedback.* Actually, returns can be a huge source of market research for a business. Even if a no-hassle return policy is in place, asking customers for feedback on the reason for return can provide valuable insight for changing products and services offered. A lot of *"changed my mind"* or *"no reason"* responses could indicate a higher incidence of unscrupulous returns.

Dealing with Consulting Freebies and Scope Creep

Returning a product is relatively easy. Returning a service? Not so much. While many companies have customer satisfaction guarantees, on services, it needs to be clearly defined what is refundable and what is not.

Nowhere is this more difficult than in the area of consulting. A consultant can provide services and clients can say that they didn't like what was done, refusing to pay. Like the party dress example discussed earlier, these clients are *"trying on"* a consultant. Because services can't be resold like returned products might be, *"returns"* on consulting can quickly put a consultant out of business.

Consultants can easily slip into servitude mode as a reflex action when a customer expresses displeasure with this or that aspect of the consulting experience. Fearing that they will lose either the sale or the customer, they flip into *"whatever it takes"* mode to keep the business, eroding any profit margin to be earned. This also can detract attention from any other business on the agenda, increasing the potential for those engagements to go wrong, too.

What's a consultant to do?

- ***Get Everything Upfront.*** There are three things that a consultant needs upfront before engaging any customer: 1) Non-refundable deposit; 2) Contract or quote clearly defining responsibilities of both parties and work to be done; and, 3) Liquidated damages clause which defines how much is owed by a customer if a contract is cancelled.

- **Go Into "Do Not Disturb" Mode.** Until a project is officially contracted, consultants should adopt a *"no phone calls/email/meetings"* policy with customers. These communications can quickly and easily end up being consulting freebies, sometimes even being just enough advice for the client to swipe the information and do it on their own (or with a cheaper, competing consultant). Result? The consultant never gets hired or paid.

- **Remember Analysis is Consulting.** One of the difficult things that consultants run into when creating proposals is the analysis question: *How much analysis of the customer problem should be included in the proposal?* Answer: *Not much.* Define the issue to be solved, but don't analyze it. Analysis is a highly valued skill at the core of the consulting process. Build the analysis time and the talent into the proposal!

- **Watch for Scope Creep.** In the contract, parameters for phone consultations and other communications during the project should be defined so that the possibility of scope creep is reduced or eliminated. Scope creep occurs when massive changes or additional services are requested and expected by a customer without accompanying changes and additions to the contract. Again, adopting a *"Do Not Disturb"* policy, except for as outlined in the contract, can keep this in check.

CHAPTER 27:
3 Fs to Becoming a Stronger Competitor

How did you pick your current CPA or tax advisor? Did you ask about their knowledge of particular GAAP technicalities? I know I didn't. Actually, it was a referral from a family friend. Been one of the best business decisions I've made to date.

How about your plumber? Or hair stylist? Did you ask for their scores on licensing exams? Grade point average? Of course not. Chances are, like my CPA, you chose them on referral or from getting to know them in the community. These days, you might have even gotten to know them through social media.

The friend factor in competitive analysis should not be taken lightly. People often choose vendors, in both their personal and professional lives, based on referral, familiarity and friendship.

So can you claim this as a competitive advantage? Sure. Should you be developing this competitive advantage at every turn? Absolutely! Why? Because people will more likely choose a vendor they know, like and trust over a talented unknown any day. Remember when we talked about the power position of incumbent vendors?

The world is filled with extremely talented—and starving—artists, musicians and even hairstylists and plumbers that no one knows. They're just waiting to be *"discovered."* They are operating under the misguided notion that talent, knowledge and skill can be easily evaluated and found by paying customers. Know, like, trust and being easy to find trumps talent any day of the week.

So in your analysis of competitors, evaluate their friend factor against yours. If your competitor is well known in the community and has a "following," you better start building your "fan club" right away.

Networking, blogging, social media, speaking, going to events, volunteering in the community—all of these are ways to build your friend factor in the markets you want to serve. Each one of these efforts is a subject for another book. But in short, always be on the lookout for opportunities to get yourself **FRIENDED, FAMOUS AND FOUND**—the 3 Fs to becoming a stronger competitor for longer.

Going Forward

As we come to a close, I'd like to review some of the core strategies for dealing with competition in business that we have been discussing.

First of all, know yourself, know your business and where you fit in the market landscape. Secondly, you need to know your competition, the obvious and the not so obvious. Next, you need to adopt a keep in touch, keep it friendly strategy with your clients that are a really good fit for you, but maybe the buying timing or situation just isn't right. And lastly, you want to keep filling your business pipeline with new leads and new prospects, because that is the only way to build your business for the future.

Again, thank you for the time you've spent with me, and good luck as you find your business competitive advantage.

Heidi Thorne

About Heidi Thorne

Dr. Heidi Thorne, MBA/DBA, is an author and business speaker who focuses on small business and marketing topics. She has over 25 years of experience in sales, advertising, marketing and public relations, including a decade in the hospitality and trade show industries. As well, she was a trade newspaper editor for over 15 years, has blogged since 2010 and taught at the college level for five years.

Books. Heidi has written several books and eBooks on business and self publishing. For a current listing of all books, with links to purchase, visit the "Books" page at HeidiThorne.com.

Speaking. Need a speaker for your business event? Let Heidi engage and entertain your audience! For video previews and current topics, visit the "Speaking" page at HeidiThorne.com.

www.ingramcontent.com/pod-product-compliance
Lightning Source LLC
Chambersburg PA
CBHW051323170526
45166CB00002B/659